LONG WALK TO LAVENDER STREET

A Story From South Africa

Look out for other titles in the Survivors series:

Boxcar Molly – A Story From the Great Depression

Broken Lives – A Victorian Mine Story

The Enemy – A Story From World War II

Only a Matter of Time – A Story From Kosovo

The Star Houses – A Story From the Holocaust

The Water Puppets – A Story From Vietnam

SURVIVORS

LONG WALK TO LAVENDER STREET

A Story From South Africa

Belinda Hollyer

HODDER
Wayland

an imprint of Hodder Children's Books

Book editor: Katie Orchard
Map illustrator: Peter Bull

Published in Great Britain in 2002 by Hodder Wayland
An imprint of Hodder Children's Books Limited

British Library Cataloguing in Publication Data

Hollyer, Belinda
Long Walk to Lavender Street: A Story From South Africa –
(Survivors)
1. South Africa – History 2. Children's stories
I. Title
823.9'14 [J]

ISBN 0 7502 3637 X

Typeset by Avon Dataset Ltd, Bidford-on-Avon, Warks
www.avondataset.com

Printed and bound in Great Britain by
Clays Ltd, St Ives plc

Introduction

Until the late 1960s, District Six in Cape Town was a lively multi-ethnic community of more than 60,000 people. It was primarily an area where Coloured people lived – that is, the broad community of people who were classified under South Africa's apartheid laws as being neither white, nor black African. But District Six was also home to many different ethnic groups. Coloured, Indian, black, and even white families lived there together.

District Six had a centuries-long history of cultural richness, and the relationships that flourished there were unique in South Africa under apartheid. It was a poor and overcrowded place and the living conditions were difficult, but the sense of community was strong. Its liveliness infected the whole of Cape Town. Many District Six residents had lived there for five or six generations: nowhere else was home. There was nowhere else like it.

The South African government's Group Areas Act of 1966, however, changed that for ever. The government intended to secure and extend its apartheid laws, and make sure that the minority of white people in South Africa continued to control the country. And the Group Areas Act showed the white government's determination to reserve certain areas for specific ethnic groups. Nearly every major South African town saw the uprooting of people from mixed areas, and their segregation into separate townships.

Because of its position on the doorstep of Cape Town, the land in District Six was considered too valuable to be allocated to any group other than whites. In February 1966, District Six was formally declared an area for white settlement. Everything was to be razed to the ground, and the residents re-housed within their separate ethnic groups. For all except the whites, that meant the desolate sandy wastes of the Cape Flats. For many black Africans, it could also mean being forced to move far from the Cape, to the so-called black 'homelands'.

Although the bulldozers soon moved in, years of defiant protest and court action slowed down the wholesale destruction of District Six, and prevented the rebuilding program from ever taking place. Many evicted families hung on to the shreds of their past and lived on in the ruins of their community: the last left in 1976. Today the area is still largely an open wasteland. It is a monument to the cruelty and stupidity of the apartheid system.

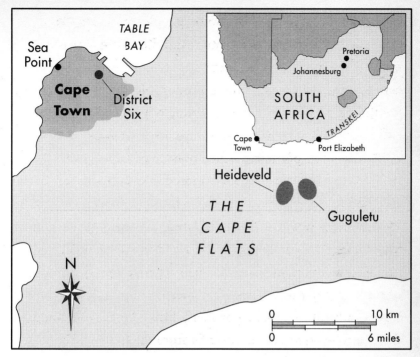

This map shows the location of District Six in Cape Town. It also shows the townships of Heideveld and Guguletu, and the distances that Siesie's family had to travel each day to get to school and work.

Acknowledgements

I would like to thank Linda Fortune, Education Officer of the District Six Museum in Cape Town; Professor Crain Soudien, of the University of Cape Town; Yousef Rassool, retired District Six resident, historian and teacher; and George Johannes, deputy High Commissioner of the South African High Commission in London for their generous help with the research for this book.

There was no Lavender Street in District Six. I have imagined that it ran parallel to Tennant Street as an extension to Godfrey Street, going up towards Chapel Street.

Siesie Ngaba and her family are also invented, but they are as true as fictional characters can be. Their story is based on fact. Everything that happens to them did happen, to thousands of people, in apartheid South Africa. This book is dedicated to those people.

One

Write It Down, Siesie

Last night there was a knock on my door, and when I opened it Joseph was standing there grinning at me. My little brother! Well, he's not so little any more – I'm tall enough, but he towers over me now. I had no idea he was in Cape Town, but that's Joseph for you. You never did know where he was, unless he wanted you to.

So we sat right down and talked, catching up on all the family news, and my daughters came by and joined in, too. We ended up having a great get-together, everyone telling stories and asking for new ones, and singing old songs, way into the night. And just before Joseph left – big government man that he is now, he had meetings early the next day up north – we stood in the warm starry dark out by the gate. Joseph hugged me because he could see that our talk had made me sad. All those bad times flooding back again. I don't think about them much any more, but they still hurt when I do.

'Write it down, Siesie,' he said. 'You remember it best of all of us, and there's a story to tell. We were rainbow people before the rainbow nation of our new South Africa was ever born – remember that. Remember Lavender Street! Remember the good times, eh – and be happy.'

Well, I do remember the good times, though I'll have to tell the bad times too. But the good times came first, so I'll start with them. And, oh! They were the *best* of good times. Back in Lavender Street, way back when I was just thirteen years old . . .

Our family lived in District Six, in Cape Town. Number 12, Lavender Street. I still live in Cape Town, but not in District Six – no one lives there any more. It's just empty waste ground, with the mosques and churches standing up like guards with no one left to watch over. To look at it now, you'd never know what we had. You'd have to look inside our hearts to see what it was like. But I'll tell you what I remember.

I remember a morning in 1966, just before it all started to go wrong. It was a Sunday in February. I woke up before Sophie and Lizzie, my sisters, and lay still so as not to disturb them – all three of us slept together in one big bed, and my two brothers, Joseph and James, slept in a bunk out on the landing. I watched the sunshine push through the cracks in the blind, and listened to the street outside. Even that early I could hear footsteps on the pavement, busy feet in Sunday shoes. And I knew they were going to my Aunt Lily's down the street, to buy her *koe'susters* – sweet sticky pieces of dough, deep-fried and then dipped in sugar syrup and fresh grated coconut. No one made *koe'susters* like Aunt Lily – not then, and not now. Eat them warm, straight from the paper cone she served them in, and your mouth thought it had gone to heaven. Aunt Lily's family was Muslim, and had their holy day on Friday. That meant they could sell *koe'susters* on Sunday mornings to the Christians, before *they* went to church. I knew she'd give me one if I went along to see her.

There were five of us kids and our parents in that tiny house. Two little rooms downstairs, two upstairs. There was no bathroom, but there was a lavatory in the back yard, and we washed every day in the kitchen sink with water we carried in from the cold tap out the back. (We all went to the Hanover Street baths on Saturday nights and queued up for five minutes each in the tub. Mumma used to bath us in twos and threes, to save money!)

I always knew Dad was black and Mumma was

coloured – I was proud of them both. As I saw it, we had the best of two worlds. Dad's family was Xhosa, from the Mbele clan, and they lived in Caledon Street, just four streets away from us. We loved going there and playing with our black cousins, and we loved going down our street to Mumma's coloured family, too. Mumma came from an old Cape Malay family and she had relatives all over Cape Town, but her close family lived in District Six.

To us, Mumma and Dad were – just Mumma and Dad. The best parents anyone could have, warm and loving, always quick to joke and play, always slow to anger. We were a very happy family. We never understood the danger we were in, or what could happen to us all.

That morning in February I slid quietly out of bed and pulled on my dress. I was just creeping out the bedroom door when I saw that little Lizzie was awake and peeping over the bedcovers at me. I knew she'd make a fuss if I didn't take her with me, so I put my finger to my lips and then beckoned her to come. She was up and had her dress on before I had tiptoed downstairs. Then she followed me down like she always did, by bumping down backwards from stair to stair – a sort of rocking crawl she'd invented herself. We were so impressed by her speed at this that we used to get her to do it for visitors, to show off our baby sister!

We walked down the street – Lizzie could just about walk by then if she had a hand to keep her steady – and then slipped down the side of Aunt Lily's house to skip the queue and get around to the kitchen, where the glorious cooking smells came from. Aunt Lily was fishing a fresh batch of *koe'susters* out of the syrup pan, but she put them aside to hug us, and then wrapped some up for us to take home for the family.

'Tell your Mumma I want to talk to her,' she called after us. 'Ask her to come by this afternoon if she can. Say I've heard we're going for white, for certain.'

I didn't know what she meant, but when I gave the message to Mumma I saw her face tighten and close up, as though she was trying not to show how she felt. It scared me when Mumma looked like that, but when I asked her what was wrong, she smiled at me and said it wasn't anything. Then the others came down to the kitchen and we ate the *koe'susters* while they were still warm, and I forgot what Aunt Lily had said, until night-time.

By then Mumma had talked to Aunt Lily, and when Dad came home – he'd been out all day helping a friend to fix a leaking roof – I heard Mumma tell him they needed to talk. Something about a Group Areas Act. I didn't understand what she meant. And when I did, I wished I'd never had to.

We were too young to understand about apartheid; what it meant and how cruel the government of our country was, back then. Oh, we knew some things. We knew Dad had to carry a special pass all the time and that Mumma didn't; and we knew lots of things were extra hard for Dad just because he was black. I always sensed that Mumma worried about him in a way that she never did about us children – as if, somehow, he was in some special kind of danger. He was, too, but I didn't know it then.

The thing was, according to the law, Mumma and Dad shouldn't really have got married at all – just because Dad was black, and Mumma wasn't. But the law about what the government called mixed marriages wasn't usually enforced unless one of the people was white. Since Dad was black and Mumma was coloured the authorities weren't bothered, even though their marriage was unusual for those times.

I won't pretend that Dad's family and Mumma's family were exactly pleased when their children fell in love. Dad's family was Methodist and Mumma's was Muslim, and both sets of parents wanted their children to marry inside their own religions. And they were worried about what might happen to them in the future because of the apartheid government. Everyone knew life would be harder for them both if they married each other. Before she died, Mumma told me how *her* mother had tried to stop her marrying Dad.

'Your grandma told me it would be very difficult,' said Mumma. 'She said that black people had such a hard time in South Africa, much harder than coloured people and the Lord knew that was bad enough. She said that some of that hardship would rub off on me if I married Samuel. Of course, I knew that, but I didn't care, I just loved your dadda so much I wanted to be with him, no matter what. And then she told me that if there was ever a tug between the two families, I wouldn't know whose side to take. I just looked her firmly in the eye and said: "But I do know, Ma. I'll take Samuel's side, just like you always take *your* husband's. And he'll take mine, like my father takes *yours!*" And you know, Siesie, that's what we always did, your dadda and me. We stuck together.'

By the time the five of us children came along everything had settled down and there were no serious disagreements between Mumma and Dad's families. We played with our cousins and we were always in and out of each other's houses, all over District Six. I liked Aunt Lily best out of Mumma's family, but out of all our relatives I loved Dad's brother, my uncle Jimmy, most of all because he always had time to talk to me. He told me stories about our Xhosa clan, the Mbele, and he always used my Xhosa name. I loved being called Nomvuyo – it means 'rejoice', and Dad said he had named me that because he rejoiced when I was born. I was christened Rosalta – Rosa for short, like my mother. But Mumma's family called me Siesie because I was the eldest child in the family; 'Siesie' means 'the eldest' in the Afrikaans language. And that's the name that stuck: all my brothers and sisters called me Siesie most of the time. Still do. That's OK, but I miss being Nomvuyo.

So, who did I think I was, back then? Black because of Dad, or coloured because of Mumma – or what?

You know, we just didn't think about it like that: kids aren't bothered about colour one way or another unless they're made to be. The way things were was just . . . the way things were. My Xhosa cousins went to a different school – but so did my older coloured cousins, so that didn't seem strange. And our different families spoke different languages – but that wasn't strange either, because there were so many languages in District

Six. Just in our house we spoke Afrikaans, Xhosa and English – and sometimes a mixture of all of those in one sentence! Dad could speak even more languages, but he liked speaking Xhosa and English best. My Cape Malay cousins could recite in Arabic because they learned that in the mosque, one of my friends down the road spoke Yiddish at home, and there was a German family nearby that I learned some German words from. I even knew a few Italian words from another Rosa – an Italian Rosa – who went to our school because her father was coloured.

We were lucky, of course. District Six wasn't like the rest of Cape Town, or the rest of South Africa, come to that. District Six was famous, and we were all proud to live there. We were a multi-ethnic community when the rest of the country was being divided up into ethnic groups and areas – people separated out according to their skin colour. That's how the apartheid government tried to control the country. There were so many more black and coloured people than whites in South Africa, the white authorities wanted to keep us all down so they could stay in power. Mostly coloured families lived in the District but there were some black families like Dad's and some white families, too. We were used to being a mixture.

Some people say they didn't realize how much they loved living in District Six until they had to leave – but I always knew how I felt about it, and I always loved it. My very first memory is from when I was three. I can see it all clearly now, if I close my eyes. I was sitting on our front *stoep* with baby Joseph sleeping in a basket beside me, waiting for Dad to come home. I knew Mumma was in the kitchen at the back of the house so I felt very safe, and I just sat and waited and watched all the people go by, fascinated by all the sounds and the sights. There was a group of musicians down on the corner singing and playing instruments, and people tossing them coins as they passed by. Some people stopped to listen and joined in. There were big kids playing noisy street games, and neighbours on their front *stoepe*, talking and laughing and calling out to each other. Everyone smiled and stopped to say hello to me – although I was too shy back then to say much in reply. And I remember how Dad finally turned the corner from Tennant Street and saw me, and broke into a run to get to me quicker so he could scoop me up and swing me right around, the way I loved.

I've heard people say that District Six was a slum, and dangerous – but it never seemed like that to me. If it *was* true, it never touched us. We didn't have much, but neither did anyone else, so we didn't care about that. And we were never in danger in the District. My sisters and I weren't allowed out by ourselves as much as our brothers were, but that was just how it was back then. My brothers played all over the District all day and some of the night as well, and nothing bad happened to them – not then and not there. The bad all came later, in other places.

That day in 1966 was like the end of the golden weather. Afterwards, things were never so good again, because the apartheid government had just decided that District Six would be turned into a white area. Anyone who wasn't white had to leave. No ifs, no buts – everyone had to go.

No one wanted to leave. It had been home to Mumma's family for three generations, and home to Dad's family for two. Most of our neighbours could say something similar. And the trouble was, most people had nowhere else to go. The government said we all had to move out to the townships on the Cape Flats outside Cape Town, but no one wanted to go there! The townships were dismal places, with no proper roads or schools or shops, and no transport, either.

These days, people would probably get together and

fight a government that tried to take away their homes. They'd try to vote for a different political party that would treat them better. But back then none of us *had* a vote: only white people were allowed to vote in South Africa. Of course, many people did protest, but the apartheid government was so feared by everyone, protest was hard to organize. Many people thought that if they spoke up, they'd be in even worse trouble.

Mumma and Dad were more worried than most other people in the District. There was the fact that Dad was Xhosa – black, in a country where being black meant that the whole system was stacked up against you before you even took a breath. There was also the fact that Dad was married to Mumma, a coloured woman – something that might not matter from day to day, but it was technically illegal.

And Dad had another dangerous secret, too – something I'd never known until then.

Dad worked at Harvey's Garage in District Six. I sometimes saw him there on my way home from school, sweeping up out the front, or washing cars. But at other times I didn't see him when I went past the garage. I just thought he must be in the workshop out the back. But I never wondered why.

My Dad could fix anything. He could solder up a hole

in a bucket so that you couldn't even see where the hole had been; he could make our old radio work time and again when it wouldn't get a signal, and he made the iron bedstead us three girls slept in from bits and pieces of beds he'd found in scrap heaps, and painted it to look great. He could always think through how things worked, and then make them come good again when they went wrong.

The truth was, Dad had taught himself to be a mechanic. Back then, black people weren't allowed to do certain jobs: anything that was skilled work was banned for them, because the government didn't want them to better themselves. They wanted black people to stay where they were, at the bottom of society. So black people couldn't be mechanics, and Dad had had to teach himself in secret at the garage. He used to stay on after his official hours to watch and help. The garage owner had seen how good he was and helped him to learn more. Then later on, the garage owner let Dad work as a proper mechanic – but behind closed doors, safe from prying eyes. It was hard work and long hours, but Dad liked it. As long as his real work was a secret, he could keep the job and earn a bit more money than anyone else in his family. Because Mumma worked, too, they could just manage to pay double rent on our little house.

Half the weekly payment was the basic rent and the other half went into a house purchase scheme, so that one day we would own the house and never have to pay rent again.

Money was always a problem – there was never enough, no matter what. Most weeks, just to cover that double-rent payment, we had to use some of the money set aside for food, and then Mumma had to scrape together enough to feed us all. I can remember me and my sister Sophie going down to the market before school to pick up vegetables that had fallen to the ground and couldn't be sold, so Mumma could make soup from them. You could always get marrowbones free at the butchers' and Mumma put those in soup as well. Fish heads and crayfish shells were given away in the fish market opposite the Star cinema and Mumma made a fine fish stew that way. But however short of money they were, Mumma and Dad always tried to put a little bit of cash aside to help other people when they fell on hard times. Everyone in the District knew a lot about hard times.

Now government inspectors were going to visit District Six, poking about everyone's homes and asking questions. Mumma was worried about what they'd discover. Some inspectors had come the year before, when the authorities were deciding what to do about the District. They'd meddled with things that would have been better left alone as far as everyone in the District was concerned. Mumma wasn't the only one who was worried. Lots of people feared that the inspectors would discover things about them or the way they lived. For the next few months we were all on edge, expecting the worst – but nothing happened except for lots of speculation. Eventually, the news spread down from Selkirk Street that the inspectors had started their relocation work.

'It wasn't as bad as everyone said it would be,' boasted Mumma's cousin Nazeem. He lived in Selkirk Street and had come around to tell his Lavender Street relatives all about it. 'This white man in a suit and a tie came to the door, and he knocked, you know; didn't just barge in. Quite polite.'

Mumma and Aunt Lily exchanged ironic glances. You could see they didn't rate an unknown white inspector just because he didn't barge uninvited into their houses.

'And he took a photograph of the house!' Nazeem added proudly. 'Then he came in and sat down with us and went through some forms, and asked us questions.'

'What questions, Nazeem?' asked Mumma quietly.

'About who lived in the house, and how many

people, and if they were related to each other. That sort of thing. He said the new houses out on the Flats were just for families.'

'But if that's so, what about Irene?' asked Mumma suddenly. Irene was a poor old woman who lived in the house next to Nazeem. She didn't have any family left in the world. The people in the house let her use one of their downstairs rooms. She had to get by on the kindness of her neighbours – everyone gave Irene some food from time to time, and made sure she had enough kerosene for the little stove she had in the corner of her room.

Nazeem frowned. 'I don't know,' he admitted. 'If she doesn't have family, I don't know what will happen to her.'

'Nazeem, if we *have* family we don't know what will happen to us – let alone to poor old Irene,' snapped Aunt Lily. 'You never did have much sense, and you aren't talking any now!'

Aunt Lily was right – Nazeem didn't understand. He thought it would be OK to live out on the Cape Flats, and he believed the Group Areas Inspector when he said that the first people to agree to move would get the best houses. Some other people thought the way Nazeem did. But Aunt Lily knew why Mumma was so worried.

'If Samuel's not at home, Rosa, you could – just not *say* that he's Xhosa,' I heard her murmur. 'How will the inspector know if you don't tell him, eh? He'll think what you want him to think.'

I could see that Mumma didn't like that suggestion. She never wanted to pretend that Dad was anything other than who he was – she was proud of him just as he was, she always said. Still, I think she might have followed Aunt Lily's advice, to protect Dad.

But three months later, when the inspector came to Lavender Street, Dad was at home.

Two

Show Me Your Pass, Boy . . .

Joseph and I had just got back from school – Joseph had just started at Trafalgar High School and it was my third year there. James and Sophie went to St Mark's primary school in Tennant Street. Little Lizzie didn't go to school yet, so Aunt Lily minded her in the daytime if Mumma was at work. (Mumma had a cleaning job and she worked shifts, so she often wasn't home when we got back from school.) If Lizzie was with Aunt Lily I picked her up after school, and looked after her until Mumma got back. I had to keep an eye out for the others, too, being the eldest. James and Sophie were supposed to go to Aunt Lily's place after school and wait for me, but more often they went off with their friends and came home later. No one worried about them. All the District Six kids played together, and if anyone had got hurt or was in trouble, there would always be an adult around to help.

But that day, Dad was at home when we got back. Sometimes he used to work through the weekend and then have a day off at the beginning of the week when the garage wasn't so busy. None of us liked that much because he couldn't spend time with us at the weekend when we didn't have school. If he could, he'd take us down to Woodstock Beach on Saturdays, or we'd go fishing with him and Uncle Jimmy, or we'd just visit family.

But it was lovely to have Dad waiting when we got back from school. It was a real novelty, and he always had something ready for us to eat when we came in. Oftentimes he made *umvubo* for us, which is an African dish made from mealies mixed with creamy soured milk. Then Joseph and I would sit and eat with him, and tell him about school. Dad loved to hear about the high school. He'd only gone to school for two years and he'd just about had to teach himself to read and write. He knew there was a lot he'd missed out on. There was nothing he wanted more for his children than a good education. 'You can do anything you want if you've had a good schooling, Nomvuyo,' he'd say. 'No one can hold you back if you've been right through school.'

That day, Joseph was in the middle of telling Dad

about his maths lesson – Joseph loved maths; he was really good at school then – when there was a knock at the door.

I knew immediately that something was wrong. No one knocked on doors in District Six. If the door was closed, family and friends would just open it and walk right in – they'd call out as they opened the door, and then look from room to room until they found you. On Saturday mornings, even the landlord who came for the rent didn't knock – he stood on the doorstep and called out, and then we asked him to come in and sit down while he wrote out a receipt for our money.

Our door was usually open when we were home, but there was a cold wind that day so Dad had closed it. Joseph stopped talking, and we all looked at each other. Then Dad got up and walked across to the door. Joseph and I could see out the door from where we sat at the table.

A white man was standing there. He was very official looking, dressed in a suit and tie, and wearing a hat as well. He was holding a leather briefcase under his arm.

It's hard to explain how we felt when we saw him – to young people today who didn't grow up as we did, and who have never felt the fear we had for the government. We knew they could do just about whatever they liked to us, and they ruled us through that fear.

So when we saw that man standing on our *stoep*, it wasn't just that we saw something unusual – a white man from outside the District come to see us. We sensed authority, and we were worried about what that might mean.

The man said he was from the Group Areas Board office in Burg Street and he had come to get some information. I didn't like the way he talked to Dad, and I knew Dad didn't either, although he stayed as quietly courteous as ever. But the man spoke to Dad as though he was a child to be patronised, of no account at all, even calling him 'boy'. I had heard that this was how most white people behaved with black people, but I had never seen it before. It made me feel sick and frightened. I glanced at Joseph and I could see him shaking and trying not to cry. It's terrible for a child to watch someone humiliating their beloved father, and not be able to do a thing to stop it.

'Let's start with your pass, boy,' said the inspector to Dad. He meant the document that all black people had to carry with them all the time, and which showed if they were allowed to be where they were, or if they were there illegally. The man sounded easy and relaxed, like it was all nothing to him.

Dad's pass showed his job at the garage – but it didn't mention his real job there, it just said he was a cleaner. The inspector glanced through the pass, made some notes and tossed it back to Dad. Then he asked to see all our birth certificates, and the rent book – 'and your girl's pass, too, boy,' he added. By 'girl', he meant my mother.

Dad didn't explain that Mumma didn't have a pass book because she wasn't black, he just got the wooden box from the drawer where important papers were kept and took out some documents, including his and Mumma's marriage certificate. The man noted down details, raising his eyebrows when he looked at the certificate. He studied me and Joseph then; you could tell he was trying to decide if we looked more like Mumma or like Dad.

Joseph and I just sat there. We didn't say anything. Part of that was manners: Mumma and Dad had drummed into us to be polite to all grown-ups, no matter what, and that meant not speaking unless we were spoken to. I had never been so glad of that rule before; it meant we didn't have to say anything to this man who treated our father like dirt.

His visit didn't take that long: maybe half an hour. Thirty minutes that changed our lives for ever.

Three

Mamphela's Home Is Capetown

Not much happened for months, although rumours spread through the District. People in Johnson Street were already moving, went one story, and their homes were going to be pulled down. I couldn't believe the part about pulling the houses down – the ones in Johnson Street were good ones, why pull them down? But Mumma said it was most likely true.

'This government wants white folk to live here,' she said, 'but that doesn't mean they're going to live in our houses. Why would rich people live without running water or electricity, in leaky old buildings that the landlords just prop up instead of doing repairs? No, Siesie, they'll replace our little homes with big new ones, I'm sure of it. What a waste, eh? Why not just fix *our* houses up a bit, and let us stay?'

That's when Mumma's family called everyone

together. They all met at Aunt Lily's because that was the biggest house, and Mumma and Dad went along to talk about the Group Areas Act, and what the family should do. When they came back Dad was very quiet but Mumma was spitting tacks with anger – I'd never seen her so cross. It seemed that her family didn't want to stand up against the government. Many of them thought they could get better places in one of the new housing estates out in the townships.

'They're crazy!' muttered Mumma at the stove, stirring the soup so fiercely she almost turned the pot over. 'They'll never get anywhere as good as here. After they've left they'll realize that, but it will be too late! Too late for everyone!'

Mumma was right, of course. A community isn't just the place where you live – it's much more than that. Before that wicked law was passed to make everyone leave District Six we lived surrounded by warmth and friendship, with jobs and neighbours, shops and schools close by. Now all that was to be swept away.

Dad's family had their own meeting – the elders of the Mbele clan got together to discuss the situation. Dad and Uncle Jimmy were both elders. But there was nothing they could do about what was happening. It was the first time I really saw the gulf that existed between my parents' families. At least Mumma's family could *try* to fight if they chose to. Dad's family couldn't even choose. They had no rights at all.

Black people were now being forced out of Cape Town. Most of Dad's Xhosa friends were contract labourers in Cape Town where the work was, but their families couldn't get permission to live in the city, too. They only saw each other for a week at Christmas.

It was around this time that Uncle Jimmy's wife, my Aunt Mamphela, had such bad times with the authorities. She was Xhosa, too, and Uncle Jimmy's pass allowed him to be in Cape Town because he had a job. Mamphela wasn't supposed to live with him – her pass wasn't endorsed for Cape Town. But Mamphela refused to leave her husband.

First, the authorities forced her to leave the house where Uncle Jimmy lived, so Mamphela went out to one of the squatter camps with some of her friends. The women made homes there as best they could; shacks, made from old boards and plastic sheeting. Mamphela visited Jimmy whenever she could, and Jimmy went to see her when he wasn't working. But then the authorities said the squatter camp was illegal, too. Mamphela and her friends were arrested and told they would have to go 'home' to the Transkei.

'Home!' snorted Dad when Uncle Jimmy told him about this latest development. 'That's not our home! They say we have a homeland in the Transkei as if they're giving the Xhosa people a present. But I've never been to the Transkei, nor have you, Jimmy, and neither has Mamphela. None of our family has *ever* been there. Mamphela's home is in Cape Town, where she was born.'

The police forced Mamphela and her friends on to a bus, and sent them right across South Africa to the edge of the Transkei. More police were waiting for them at the other end. But when the bus got there the women refused to get off! They just sat there singing. In the end the policemen brought dogs on to the bus to make them get off, and *still* those women wouldn't do what they were told. They did get off the bus, in the end – but then they just picked up their bundles and started walking back to Cape Town. That time, the police gave up. And the women got back to the western Cape, and built more shacks in a different place.

Mamphela's courage and steadfastness taught me how it was, being black in South Africa. I realized that if Mumma had been black like Dad we would all be registered as black as well, and the authorities could have split up our family at any time.

I didn't know that it could happen anyway.

Four

Waiting To Move

After a while we got used to hearing the rumours about what was happening to District Six, and since a lot of it turned out not to be true we stopped paying so much attention. So the first thing that shocked me into realizing what was really going on, was when my best friend at school just – disappeared.

One day Linda and I had been in class as always, sitting together at our double desk and testing each other's spelling at lunchtime. We were taught in Afrikaans for some lessons and in English for others, and my English spelling wasn't as good as Linda's. She was very patient at helping me with it.

The next day Linda wasn't at school. I wondered why not, because Linda was never sick, but no one knew anything. The seat next to me stayed empty all day. She still wasn't there the day after. Just as I was planning to go to Linda's house after school and see her, our teacher told me to clear out Linda's desk and give her all the books.

I just stared at her.

'Rosalta Ngaba, please do as I say!' said Mrs Fischer briskly. So I did, and when I handed in Linda's books I asked the teacher what was wrong with Linda. I remember imagining that she must be *very* sick, maybe she'd had to go into hospital . . .

'Linda's family has been moved to Manenburg,' said Mrs Fischer. 'She won't be coming back to Trafalgar High.'

Manenburg was one of the coloured townships out on the Cape Flats. Linda hadn't said anything about it the day before, so she couldn't have known then: she would have told me. Why had the move happened so fast? I met Linda by chance, just five years ago, at a union meeting in Cape Town. She told me then how she'd got home from school and seen the entire contents of her house piled up in a lorry out the front. Men had arrived that morning with the keys for an apartment out in Manenburg, and an army lorry to transport them there. The men had wanted to take everything then and there, but Linda's mother made them wait until the children came home from school, so they could all leave together for their new home. Imagine if the men had refused to wait: imagine if you got home from school one day to find your home packed up and gone!

The Manenburg apartment had been so bad that they had only stayed a week. Then, Linda's mother had taken her children off to live with an aunt in Port Elizabeth. Linda had never seen the District again in all those years, and when I drove her down after the meeting to look at what had been done to it, she burst into tears.

Anyway, I got back from school that day wanting to talk to Mumma about Linda's disappearance. Mumma was at home when I got there, and so were Aunt Lily and her husband, Yusef – but they were all too busy talking about what had happened to Nazeem's family to listen to me. Like us, Nazeem's family paid double rent on their house. Salim, Nazeem's father, had just heard that when they were moved out of the District, he wouldn't get any compensation for the house purchase payments he had made for so many years.

'Salim just about blew a gasket!' Uncle Yusef was saying. 'And I don't blame him, either. He's been paying for ten years now, and he'd have owned his house in another ten. Now he won't ever own it, and they say he won't get a bean back, either.'

I didn't usually bother to listen to Mumma and her

family when they were talking. But this was different. We'd been paying house purchase money, too. Would we lose all our payments as well?

'What does the landlord say?' Mumma was asking.

Uncle Yusef shrugged expressively. 'What *can* he say, Rosa?' he asked. 'It's not his fault. It's this government. Again!'

The following Saturday morning, Mumma and Dad both arranged to be at home when our landlord came for his rent money, so they could talk to him about their house purchase payments. Our landlord, Mr Kelker, promised to do what he could to help. And just because it might not be as bad as they feared, Dad was really pleased.

'You see, Rosa, the worst doesn't always happen,' said Dad, smiling and giving Mumma a hug. 'We can hope and we can pray, and who knows, eh? In the end only God knows. We haven't even been told to move, yet, remember.'

I could see that Mumma wasn't hopeful, but she did try not to think the worst. And she cheered up when she heard that some of her family were going to protest about the forced removals after all. 'You can't just give in to everything,' she said to me. 'Even if you don't stand much chance of winning, you have to try to fight against things that are really wrong. And our home – and the District – are worth fighting for, aren't they?'

Five

We'll Do Anything To Stay Together

But then something much worse happened. It made the fight a different one for my parents – for all of us.

An official letter from the Group Areas Board office arrived at our house. It came when Mumma was home but Dad was still at the garage. I was helping Mumma get dinner ready – Joseph was out with his friends, and Sophie and James were playing upstairs. A letter was a novelty, so I was interested to see what it was about.

Mumma opened it and read it, and then she gave a terrible sort of moaning gasp. She stood there swaying, and clutching the paper so hard it crumpled in her hand. I thought she was going to faint.

'Mumma, what's wrong?' I said, alarmed. I helped her on to the kitchen stool and poured her a glass of water, but she didn't stop clutching that letter against her.

'Mumma, tell me! What is it?'

Mumma took a deep breath, and squared her shoulders in the way that she did when she had to tackle something very hard.

'Siesie, darling, listen to me. You're going to have to be very brave, and help me bear this. We can't tell the little ones yet, but you'll have to know. I can't think what to do . . .'

Another pause, and another deep breath. By now I had my arms around her, and tears were running down my face. I still didn't know what was wrong but I had never seen Mumma behave like this in the whole of my life. I couldn't bear to see her distress.

'The letter – that man who came to see your dadda – this letter is from his office. It says we have a place in the coloured township at Heideveld. But the letter says Samuel can't live there.'

I stared at Mumma's face. I still didn't get it.

'Your dadda can't live with us when we leave District Six,' Mumma said again, in a shaky voice.

'But, Mumma . . . that can't be true.'

'It's true, Siesie, darling. It *is* true. I'll have to tell Samuel when he gets home. It will break his heart to be apart from us all. I'll have to find a way to help him bear this, and look for a way around it, too.' Mumma held me close. 'Help me to help him,' she said.

'It's because Dad's Xhosa, isn't it?' I knew it in my heart, but I needed to hear it out loud.

'It's because the government wants to divide people up into groups based on their colour,' Mumma said bitterly. She smoothed out the letter and looked at it again. 'That's what this is all about, Siesie. They won't stop until they've got everyone under their thumb – everyone in the whole of South Africa controlled and confined. They say I can have a place in Heideveld because I am registered as coloured, and you children are as well. Your father and I decided to do that before you were even born, to give you better schooling and better chances in life. But your dadda is black, and so they say he must go into a hostel for single men in one of the black townships.'

'But, Mumma,' I said, 'how can they split us up? We're a family! You and Dad are married! Everyone knows that. They can't do it – why would they want to do such a thing? Can they truly *make* us?'

Mumma looked at me again, and by now she was crying, too. 'They can make us if they want to,' she said. 'They can do almost anything they like. But don't you think for a moment that we won't fight it, Siesie. We'll do anything we can to stay together as a family.'

I didn't realize just how brave Mumma was even to

think of taking on the apartheid government, but she always was a tiger if she thought anyone was trying to hurt her family. Later, I learned how much courage it took to challenge anything that the government did, and how much danger that brought with it: danger of harassment and intimidation, imprisonment, and even death. Back then I only knew my misery at the idea of losing my father, and my confusion at wondering how we would all cope without him. And how much he would miss us.

Dad was a quiet and gentle man who took life seriously. Most of the time he looked solemn, and you might have thought he didn't smile or laugh easily if you didn't know him well. But with Mumma, or when any of us came back to the house from school or from playing with our friends, the smile of delight that lit up his face told us everything we needed to know. Now that I look back on my memories of Mumma and Dad, too, I can see how good they were for each other. Mumma's emotions were closer to the surface than Dad's were, and Dad mostly took longer to come to a conclusion about something than Mumma did. But they worked in such harmony together with us kids, and their respect and love for each other shone through them both like a beacon.

I was lucky to have them to learn from.

That night was the hardest time I'd ever had in all my life. We had to get through feeding James and Sophie and Lizzie and putting them to bed, and then through homework time for Joseph and me. Joseph sensed that something was wrong, but he didn't know what it was and kept trying to get it out of me. All the time, Mumma behaved as though it was just another ordinary night, not showing a thing to the little ones or to Dad when he came in.

She told him after we were all in bed. I was lying awake in the dark listening to Lizzie and Sophie breathing and wondering what was going on and what would happen. I heard Mumma's voice low downstairs, and then an anguished shout from Dad, as though he had been struck. Then nothing. I crept out on to the landing and saw Joseph out of his bunk bed, hunched up shivering in the dark at the top of the stairs.

'*Now* will you tell me what's wrong?' he hissed. 'I heard Dad shout out, and now it sounds like he's crying, and Mumma's crying, too. What's it about, Siesie? You *have* to tell me!'

So I did. I was too upset myself to choose my words carefully, and I always think that if I'd done a better job that night, then Joseph wouldn't have gone the way he did. He was so shocked and frightened, that at first he refused to believe me. He shouted at me in a voice husky with rage and grief, saying, 'No! No! That can't be true!' Then he ran downstairs, out the front door and away up the street, before anyone could stop him. Oh, he came back – hours later, after Dad had searched the streets for him – but by then something had turned around in his mind, and he wouldn't even say he was sorry for doing it. He stood sullenly in front of Mumma and Dad while they both talked sternly to him. The old Joseph would have done anything he could to get back in their good books. This new closed-up Joseph just silently hung his head when they talked to him, and in the end they sent him back into the bunk with James (who had slept through the whole thing).

It was then, when things started to go wrong for us all, that they first went so hard for Joseph.

Years later when we were grown up, I asked Joseph about it. And he said it had been the sheer shock of thinking he was losing Dad, and the rage he'd felt that anyone could take his father away from him. 'The injustice of it, Siesie, that was what got me,' he said. 'I didn't have words for it, and I didn't know what to do with the pain. It went deep, like a knife wound. I was angry with everyone, and I felt powerless – I was angry about that, too. I just lashed out at everything.'

Six

'Enkosi, Tata'

Mumma and Dad discussed the letter with their families, of course, and tried to work out what they could do about it. There was talk of hiring a lawyer, but that kind of money was more than they could afford to spend or borrow – especially with the worry about losing the house payments hanging over their heads. And they knew that the law wasn't on their side.

In the end, they braved the Group Areas Board office together. Mumma was dead against that idea; she didn't think anything good would ever come out of that building. 'What makes you think the *Boere* will ever give a black person the chance to argue their case?' she asked. But Dad had worked out what he wanted to say, and he just wanted a chance to talk to someone who might listen. So he got all his courage together, he and Mumma took time off work, and down they went in their best clothes, to sit for hours in the Burg Street office waiting to talk to an inspector. But when they finally got to see one of the men, he just dismissed all their arguments in a minute; didn't want to listen to Dad and called him '*kaffir*', which was even worse than being called 'boy'. So Dad knew he couldn't take his protests any further. He guessed that the office might revoke his pass and make it impossible for him even to stay in Cape Town if he did anything else. Uncle Jimmy and two of his cousins had just had their passes challenged by the police, and it looked as though they would be sent away, too, just like Aunt Mamphela. Everywhere we turned at that time, someone we knew was under attack.

I remember talking to Dad just after he'd been so badly treated in the Group Areas Board office. He and I were sitting on our front *stoep* together, watching Sophie and her friends play hopscotch. I asked him what he thought would happen to us all, and he smiled gently at me and put his arm around my shoulders.

'Don't worry, Nomvuyo,' he said. 'God sends troubles to everyone, but he seems to send more to black people in our South Africa, than to the white ones. Sometimes I believe that poor Job in the Bible must have been a black man, too.'

I'd heard the story of Job in Sunday School, how the

Bible says that he was sent a host of troubles to test his faith in God – but that Job just kept on believing in God, whatever went wrong. I looked at Dad.

'Do *you* believe that things will be OK in the end?' I asked him. He hugged me tighter.

'Now listen to me, Nomvuyo,' he said. 'These are bad times, and who's to say they won't get worse still? I believe I *am* going to have to live apart from you all: that's the way it looks, and that's the way it's likely to be. If I could change that, I would. You know that?'

I nodded, too sad to speak.

'But nothing can change the way I feel about you, Nomvuyo. You are my heart's delight. If I had to live a hundred miles away from you, or a thousand, it wouldn't change that. You and your brothers and sisters, you are all precious to me – wherever we are, and whatever happens to us. So you must be brave, and look after the others. I rely on you to help your mother, and I know you won't let me down.'

'*Enkosi, tata*,' I said in Xhosa – Thank you, Dad.

'*Enkosi*, Nomvuyo,' said Dad back, hugging me again.

And that had to do.

Before we heard exactly where we were supposed to move to, Joseph began mixing with a wild crowd of boys – mostly other kids from District Six who had no family discipline and did more or less what they wanted, with no one to tell them otherwise. They didn't necessarily do bad things – just dangerous ones that could get them into a lot of trouble with the authorities if they were caught. Joseph was still going to school with me in the mornings, but I knew sometimes he ducked out later and went off to meet his new friends. Oftentimes I'd come home by myself because Joseph was missing. No one from school seemed to know what was happening with him, but it was a hard time for many pupils and Joseph wasn't the only one acting up.

And then one evening Joseph didn't come home at all. Mostly he'd be back home for dinner, and then he'd mess around pretending to do some homework to fool Mumma – but that night he wasn't there. When nine o'clock came I told Mumma that he hadn't been at school at the end of the day – not because I wanted to get him into trouble, but because I knew this might be serious.

Mumma was angry. 'As if we didn't have enough to worry about!' she said. 'I'm tired of his bad attitude.' But she was worried, too. And when he still hadn't come home at midnight, Dad went to ask Uncle Jimmy to help look for Joseph. I was waiting up with Mumma when he returned, looking grim.

'Jimmy says there was trouble in Langa today,' said Dad. 'There was a protest meeting and a march, and the police moved in, beating up anyone who got in their way with their *sjamboks*, and arresting people. Jimmy's heard that Ray and Neville were involved, and he thinks at least one of them was arrested. And – Joseph was seen out in Langa this morning.'

Ray and Neville were two of our Mbele clan cousins. I knew Joseph liked them but I didn't know he was hanging out with them. And in Langa, too – that was a black township out on the Cape Flats filled with despair and desolation. The conditions out there were very bad. A few years earlier there had been a protest march from Langa all the way into the centre of Cape Town. More than thirty thousand black men had defied the police to march in that peaceful protest. Hundreds had been arrested and imprisoned. Some of them had been sent to Robben Island, the harsh prison out in the Cape Town bay. We all knew that anyone who was arrested in another Langa protest would be in serious trouble.

Dad explained that Uncle Jimmy had gone back out to Langa to try to get some news, and to find out if Joseph had been involved. We couldn't do anything until we knew more. You might wonder, now, why my parents didn't get on to the police about their missing boy? But you have to understand how it was in those days. The police weren't there to help us in any matter. No one thought to go and ask them if they had arrested Joseph – no black or coloured person asked the police for help back then. It wouldn't have done any good. So we all went to bed, though I don't suppose Mumma and Dad got any more sleep than I did that night.

And the news the next day was not good. Joseph *had* been among the protesters, and now the word was that he was on the run, hiding from the police who were still searching for anyone who had been involved. They were determined to crack down on people who stood out against apartheid, as a warning to everyone else.

Dad understood what Joseph had done, better than Mumma did. Mumma was distraught that any of her children should be in trouble with the police – doubly so for any political disturbance that could only end badly. But Dad saw Joseph's pain and confusion about our family troubles, and he knew that Joseph's wayward behaviour came out of that. Not that Dad wasn't cross – he always came down hard on any of us if we upset Mumma. But in his heart, I think he was proud of Joseph for standing up for what he thought was right.

I did hear him say to Mumma, 'At least the boy's not a *skollie*, Rosa.' (*Skollie* was a word for a gangster.) But Mumma asked him sharply what he thought the difference was if Joseph ended up in jail anyway, so Dad didn't say more.

Three days later, Joseph came home – thin, dirty, bruised and exhausted, but still in one piece; safe at least for now. He had been hiding in shacks around the squatter camps and the townships by day, and moving around by night whenever the people who were helping him thought it was safe. Now he could finally come home again.

Dad talked to him for hours in private. Joseph told me years later that Dad took him into his confidence, man to man, and made him feel there might be hope for us all. He told Joseph that he was proud of him for trying to fight injustice, but that he needed Joseph to help protect the family when Dad couldn't be around. He made Joseph promise he'd go to school and stay all through school hours. And Joseph was better for a while after that; he really tried to keep his promise.

After a couple more months of waiting, Mumma was told where we would be moving to in Heideveld. We didn't know what it was like and we weren't hoping for much – but when Dad was told he had to go to a hostel in Guguletu we felt more hopeful than we had for a long time. You see, Guguletu was a black township close to the coloured township of Heideveld – just a few miles further out from Cape Town. My parents had decided to do whatever it took to keep their family together. Dad would live officially in the hostel as he was supposed to, but unofficially he would spend all the time he could with us in Heideveld. And if his hostel was in Guguletu, that would make it easier for him.

We had more warning of the move than Linda's family did – we knew for months before we left District Six just where we were going. But that didn't make things easier. It was such a strange time. Everything in District Six was turning upside down. Some of the shops were closing down and many people had already left. But others had decided to hang on as long as they could, and Aunt Lily and Uncle Yusef were amongst that group. They had found a lawyer to help and were determined to stick it out for as long as possible. They offered to get their lawyer to look into our house purchase money, too. And although my parents never did get that money back, the kindness and support of Mumma's family made them feel better.

Seven

How Can We Live Like This?

All around us, the bulldozers began to move in to the emptying streets. At first this was exciting for District Six children, who'd never seen such enormous machines before. They all used to stand and watch as the bulldozers ripped into deserted houses and tore them apart – tearing our old lives to pieces at the same time, and scattering them like dust. Lots of my friends had now been moved to the townships, but most of them were coming back into school every day because there were no high schools in the townships for them. They had to travel about fifteen miles each way just to get to school. And there were no regular buses then between the townships and Cape Town; you could get a bus or a train part-way, but after that you just had to walk, or hope for a lift. It took hours. I knew Joseph and I could manage it but I wondered how James and Sophie were going to walk so far every day.

We seemed to wait for ever, suspended in a sort of melancholy limbo. From time to time news would come of more friends moving away, or more shops closing down, or another protest group's activities in the fight to stay on in the District. We couldn't be involved directly in any protest – the danger for Dad was too great.

On our last night, Dad and Mumma took us all for a walk through Cape Town. We left the streets of District Six and went right down into the city, walking for hours and visiting our favourite spots. It was a magical evening, with the air soft and warm, and everything looking so pretty and bright. Finally we walked slowly up through the Government Gardens to see all the big fancy buildings. James loved the museums; he always boasted he was going to build something bigger than any of them when he grew up. And we stopped to look at the goldfish in the art gallery fishpond because Lizzie loved *them* best – but she was asleep in Dad's arms by then, so she missed them. Sophie was so upset that Lizzie had slept through the fish that she insisted on unpacking our crayons that night and drawing Lizzie a picture of us all standing round the fishpond, with the fish as big as we were! (Believe it or not, I still have that picture somewhere; I've hung on to it all these years.)

When we finally got back to Lavender Street we sat on the floor in the front room, surrounded by the bits and pieces of our lives tied up in bags and boxes. Sophie drew her picture, Dad told us stories, and Mumma sang until after midnight. It was a very special night.

Dad left before dawn the next morning for work: he'd meet us later at Heideveld. He shouldn't still have been in District Six, and he didn't want the lorry driver to have a chance to report him. The less anyone except the family knew about our plans, the better it would be.

We had spent days packing, but Mumma and I were still up early to tie up the final bundle of bedding, and deal with breakfast. Joseph and I had taken the day off school to help Mumma, but James and Sophie went to school as usual. We'd collect them when we were ready to leave. Lizzie was spending the day with Aunt Lily, as she often did. Mumma didn't want to disrupt the little ones' lives any more than she had to. They all understood as much as they had to know: that Dad wasn't going to live with us all the time any more; and that they mustn't answer any questions about Dad if anyone asked them.

Our neighbours all came in to say goodbye and wish us good luck. We were the first to leave Lavender

Street, and they saw our departure as the beginning of the end for all of them. Our next door neighbour, Mrs Mandindi, cried as she hugged Mumma. But then the lorry finally arrived and things went from slow motion to double speed. Dad and Joseph had taken the beds apart the day before and had stacked everything neatly in the front room downstairs, even Mumma's little dressing table that she loved so much – it was an old-fashioned wooden one with carved sides, covered with little mirrors. The driver wasn't careful or respectful about our property at first, just throwing our things into the back of the lorry any old way until Mumma saw what he was doing. She spoke so sharply to him he looked embarrassed, and he went more carefully after that. Some of our things got even more battered than they were already, but nothing went missing because of Mumma's sharp eyes – she'd heard how other families had lost their belongings on lorries that went to the wrong place, or never turned up in the townships. That was why she had decided that we should all travel in the lorry, too, and keep a close watch on everything.

When we were ready, Mumma insisted that the driver sat down on the *stoep* with her and wait, while Joseph and I walked down to St Mark's to collect James and Sophie. When we got back to Lavender Street and

51

James and Sophie saw the lorry, their eyes grew round with amazement – it was bigger than any vehicle they'd ever seen in our street before. For them, climbing into the back with Joseph and me, and travelling out to Heideveld was an enormous adventure!

The journey was dusty and uncomfortable, and we had to hang on to James and Sophie all the way to stop them bouncing about – Mumma was in the front of the truck with the driver. It took more than an hour to drive to Heideveld, and the longer it took the more I wondered about getting back into Cape Town for school. Mumma was worried, too, she told me later, sitting in the front trying to work out how she could get to and from her cleaning job and look after her children at the same time. We knew it was a long way, but none of us had realized just how far away it was until we took that lorry ride.

I'd never have been able to guess how unpleasant the new place would be. Some of the new coloured townships were OK, and parts of Heideveld had really nice houses – but not our bit. We pulled up in a street of tenement buildings that seemed to have been dumped in the middle of nothing – just like us, I thought, as we scrambled down. The street wasn't paved and there weren't any streetlights – but it wasn't like out in the countryside, with trees and grass and fresh air. There was nothing but emptiness with dirt and rubbish blowing around.

James and Sophie still thought it was a huge game. They giggled with excitement as we helped the driver carry our things inside. When we had everything and the lorry had driven away, Mumma slowly looked around.

'Look at this! It's a disgrace!' she said. 'Our Lavender Street house was old and shabby, but it was a house, and it was ours. Here – what do we have? Three dirty rooms with precious little privacy and no water tap, sharing a blocked-up lavatory out the back with everyone else in the block. Look, it's a new building and there's already mould on the walls. And the government makes me pay as much for these rooms as we paid for the whole house in District Six! How can we live like this?'

It took us ages to get our rooms even halfway clean. We scrubbed the walls and the floor, and that meant walking down the road to a standpipe to get water. Sophie and James did that together, while Joseph, Mumma and I scrubbed and rinsed and then scrubbed again. By the time Dad arrived that night the rooms didn't look so bad, and they smelled a lot better. There was no electricity but we had oil lamps, and a little oil stove for cooking – we had left our big old stove behind in Lavender Street. Mumma had brought a stew in a big pot, and she heated that up for dinner. James and Sophie were so exhausted from everything they fell asleep before they'd finished eating.

Dad stayed the night, but he'd gone again the next morning before I woke up – he had to walk into Cape Town to the garage. I helped Mumma get James and Sophie up and dressed – they were sleepy and cranky and they didn't want to walk into Cape Town but there was nothing else for it: Mumma had to go to work, too, and there was nowhere else for them to go. We all trooped up to the main road to look for a bus, and I saw children from other rooms in our building playing out in the street. That worried me – if they didn't go to school, was it really hard to get there?

I was right about that.

Mumma's job was in Sea Point, which had meant taking a bus, then walking from District Six – about an hour each way. Now it would take her about three hours each way unless she got a ride into Cape Town. That first morning we shared a taxi with some other people who were waiting up on the main road, but we couldn't afford that every day. It would be too much money on top of the rent. At Lavender Street . . .

I stopped myself from making the comparison. Everything had been better in Lavender Street and it was no use looking back all the time. We had to learn to cope with how it was now, in Heideveld.

Eight

Walking – Always Walking

And we all did try very hard. Mumma talked to James and Sophie about our new situation, and they stopped complaining about being woken so early. They learned to be ready to leave with me and Joseph, once they had dressed and eaten something. I made sure they took food with them; they were too little to last so long without eating. But oftentimes they were exhausted by the time they got home: they were too tired to eat dinner and they were too tired to work at school. Sophie's teacher told Aunt Lily that Sophie was falling asleep in class. It wasn't right.

Lizzie had to live with Aunt Lily when Mumma was working. There was no one nearby in Heideveld whom Mumma could trust with her precious child. So we only saw Lizzie once or twice a week, unless we went to Aunt Lily's place after school. Aunt Lily didn't mind a

56

bit, she thought it was a treat to have a baby around again – her two boys were grown up. But I was worried that Lizzie would forget us if she hardly saw us. She was only three: wouldn't she think that Aunt Lily was her mumma if she was always with her?

Mumma found it nearly impossible to get to work on time. She tried – she got up before dawn, and if Dad had stayed over at our place she left with him before we all woke up, so they could walk into Cape Town together. Sometimes they were lucky with a bus, and very occasionally they shared a taxi with friends, but most days they walked. Then, once she got into Cape Town Mumma got a bus on out to Sea Point. She told me that even before dawn, the roads were filled with hundreds of people from the townships walking silently along, all of them trying to hold down the jobs they had, or to find work – any work at all – in Cape Town. There was no work out in the townships. Their situation was desperate.

All this meant that Mumma couldn't look after us as she had done – she wasn't there to do it. In spite of her efforts she was arriving late at work, and getting into trouble for it. She had to stay late to finish her work, and then she faced the long journey home again carrying whatever food she'd managed to buy for our evening meal: there were no shops in Heideveld. She'd arrive home grim-faced and exhausted – and then start up all over again. I tried to help but Mumma insisted that I kept on top of my schoolwork. So Mumma had to cook for her family, care for James and Sophie, keep up with the water and the washing and the fuel and the food, work out how to see Lizzie, watch out for Dad – it was truly impossible to do everything. She knew that, but she wouldn't admit it. You *can* do the impossible if you have to, for a while. And Mumma did.

But if we thought we were having the hardest of times, we soon discovered that wasn't so: Dad's situation was worse. The first Sunday we were in Heideveld was Mumma's day off and we all walked out to Guguletu to visit Dad in his hostel. We imagined him maybe lying in bed late while he waited for us – we even thought we might tiptoe into his room and surprise him sleeping.

Some parts of Guguletu are OK now, but back then there were great mounds of garbage everywhere – dirt, flies, and everywhere the stink of despair. We looked in disbelief at the building Mumma said was Dad's hostel: it was more like a cell block. Dad's room was upstairs. I say 'Dad's room', but he didn't have one to himself – he didn't even have a bunk to himself. He shared a room with six other men, and there were only four bunks.

Three of the men had their wives and children there, too – they had nowhere else to go. So the men took turns to sleep in the top bunks, curtained off with some old sheeting, while everyone else ate, talked and tried to get on with their lives in the rest of the room. There was one kitchen for the whole block, one shower, and an outside lavatory. And that was it. That was Dad's new home.

Dad was on one of the upper bunks when we arrived, but he heard us coming, pulled back the curtain, and let out a whoop of joy. The other men grinned; they understood how Dad felt about seeing us. Three of the men and their families went to sit in another bunkroom to make room for us to visit Dad. We sat on the floor and the edge of the bunks, and Dad hugged us all, and then he sat with James on his knee and Sophie draped around his shoulders, listening to Joseph talking. Then Sophie played with some of the other children, and drew pictures for Dad, and James told him one of his stories – James used to tell amazing serial stories, with a whole host of characters, that went on and on for weeks. Joseph and Mumma helped Dad set up a better system with the privacy curtains. So we all tried to make it work.

But we didn't visit Dad again.

The first weeks after we moved are just a jumbled blur. Early mornings. Trying to help Mumma. Carrying water. Doing homework by lamplight. Washing my uniform blouse at night and flapping it over the stove in the morning to dry it. Fighting with Sophie and James. And walking – always walking.

Mumma was still hanging on to her cleaning job and Joseph was still going to school, but things were bad for the little ones. I had a real battle with them in the mornings, especially if Mumma had already left for work. Sometimes I bribed them with sweets if I could get them, or with extra smears of jam on their bread when we were trying to ration food. One morning James ran off and hid and I couldn't find him. I had to take Sophie by herself and she moaned all the way to the main road, dragging her feet and lagging behind me until I thought I would go mad with frustration.

But we saw Dad whenever he could get to us, and we were still managing. Just. Just about. We were trying.

Nine

Don't Give Up, Mumma!

But then everything bad seemed to happen at once. It started when Mumma left Sophie with a woman upstairs for the day, because Sophie had been sick and wasn't yet strong enough for the long journeys. I had stayed home for three days to care for her but Mumma wouldn't let me do that any longer, and she had to get back to work herself. And the woman seemed all right; her children were the only ones in the building who kept regular hours – they even went to school sometimes. But when Mumma got home Sophie was running a fever and had been vomiting – no one had tended her. So Mumma spoke sharply to the woman.

I have always wondered if that woman reported us to the authorities, out of spite. Said that Dad was with us, instead of in the hostel.

Two days later, Mumma lost her job. The woman she

worked for lost patience with Mumma because she'd been late so often. And Mumma had taken two days off work when Sophie was sick. She'd never had to do that in District Six – there was always someone nearby who could help out.

The next day the garage owner told Dad he'd have to go part-time. The garage wasn't doing good business any more with so many people leaving District Six, and the owner had to cut back. Dad could stay, but his hours and wages would be cut almost by half.

Dad couldn't leave even if he'd wanted to – he didn't have the right to stay in Cape Town without that job, and the law gave him only seventy-two hours to find another one if he lost it. He'd just have to look around for a second job and try to make up the money.

But he didn't get a chance to do that. He got arrested instead.

Years later I discovered that my gentle father, the kindest man I've ever known, who'd never hurt anyone in his life, was thrown into a cell at the Roeland Street station and beaten up by the police. I think they might have suspected the truth about the garage job because they went for his hands first, and broke the bones in both of them – to punish him, or to stop him ever doing skilled work again: I don't know which. Then they kicked and hit him so hard all over his body that his chest and back were a mass of bruises, and his ribs were broken.

The excuse? The police said his pass wasn't in order, and they called him an "undesirable *kaffir*" – a terrible insult to a black person.

There was nothing wrong with Dad's pass, but when he said he had an approved job the police started to hit him. Then they taunted him with an offer of 'real *kaffir* work' – as a farm labourer in the Transkei.

I still believe someone told the authorities that Dad was spending time with us at Heideveld instead of in the hostel at Guguletu, and that's why the police picked him up. Or maybe it was the mechanic's job he did behind closed doors; maybe someone resented that.

But it's possible it happened for no special reason at all. Maybe it was just because Dad was black, in the wrong place at the wrong time. There's no way to tell now.

No one told us where Dad was. He just disappeared, and after a day and a night Mumma was frantic with worry. It wasn't until two days later that the garage owner heard that Dad had been picked up after he left work and got word to Aunt Lily, and she came out to Heideveld to tell Mumma. Then Aunt Lily and Uncle

Yusef went down to the Roeland Street police station with Mumma. I stayed home with James and Sophie and Lizzie. It was the longest day I'd ever known.

Mumma got home just before dawn the next morning. I found her sitting on her old kitchen stool staring at nothing.

'Your father's been deported. He's been put on an army lorry and sent to the Transkei,' she said quietly. 'They say that's sending him "home". Home—!' Mumma's voice caught on the word.

I put my arms around her. She felt so fragile suddenly, so small and defeated. I shook her gently.

'Mumma, don't give up. They can't take Dad away from us. He'll come back, like Aunt Mamphela did!' But Mumma shook her head slowly.

'I don't think he'll be able to,' she said. 'They sent him in chains. I only saw him for a moment; I couldn't even touch him. I called out to him as they dragged him into the truck but I don't think he heard me. He'd been hurt, Siesie. Badly hurt. And they'll dump him somewhere miles out in some resettlement camp, and he'll have to fend for himself amongst strangers, and he won't be able to get away. Those camps are like prisons. Now they've sent Uncle Jimmy and his brothers away, too, I don't have any way of contacting Samuel. I don't even know where I can write to him.'

I wouldn't have minded Mumma's pain so much if she'd shouted or cried, but she didn't, she just sat and stared at the wall. Like she'd gone away somewhere, too. Like the light had gone out of her.

I knew how she felt. Not seeing much of Dad was one thing; not seeing him at all and not knowing where he was, only that he was hurt and hundreds of miles away on the other side of the country – it was enough to break your heart.

And you know, I think it did break Joseph's heart. He went off the rails big-time for a long while afterwards. He came good again, but he was never the same. He's kind and loving now, but there's a bit of him missing, somehow. And it was like that with Mumma, when it happened. A bit of her went missing.

I remembered what Dad had said to me on the *stoep* at Lavender Street – how he'd love us all no matter where he was, no matter how far away – and I took some comfort from that for us, and I hoped that the thought of our love helped him, too. We found out where he'd been sent, and wrote every week to the address that Uncle Yusef's lawyer gave us, but we never heard back. It was so hard.

We had more bad times of our own. Mumma got a

job as a live-in maid in a hotel, so she could see us only one day a week, on her afternoon off. I had to look after James and Sophie by myself, so I couldn't go to school much any more. Joseph – well, Joseph left home then, if you could call the rooms in Heideveld a home. He stopped going to school, and I almost never saw him. He'd come by maybe once every couple of weeks; sometimes he'd bring money for us. I never asked where it came from, we needed it so badly.

Aunt Lily and her family were still living in Lavender Street, still fighting the District Six removals. Lizzie stayed with Aunt Lily all the time now. I was wrong to worry that she wouldn't remember us – she always did, and she was happy there. Sometimes when I saw her, my heart just about burst with aching for what we had all lost; what Lizzie would never know.

Then Aunt Lily said she'd have James and Sophie to stay as well, so they could get to school and I could go back to Trafalgar High. I resisted the idea at first; I didn't want to lose any more of my family. But then I remembered what Dad always said: I could hear his voice in my head.

'No one can hold you back if you've been right through school, Nomvuyo.'

So we accepted Aunt Lily's kind offer. And I went

back to school. I had decided to train to be a nurse, and I knew I'd have to do well at school for that.

Mumma gave up the Heideveld place. There wasn't any reason to keep it on with the little ones all at Aunt Lily's, and anyway she couldn't afford the rent and travel money without Dad's wages to help. We sold the furniture, and I lived with a school friend's family and did housework in the evenings to pay for my room and board. That gave Mumma a chance to save a little of the money she made – not much, because she needed to pay Lily for the little ones' keep. The pennies mounted up. I knew she was trying to look to the future, hoping to help Dad if she could ever find a way. Just being able to do that small thing – to save a little money where she could – calmed her anguished spirits. Gradually, Mumma started to look and sound more like herself again.

So it worked out in a way, but, oh, I was *so* lonely. All that kept me going was the hope that we could all get back together if Mumma could get a job where she could live at home again. I thought even wild Joseph might come home to us then.

I didn't know what to hope for Dad. I thought of him all the time, and Mumma and I always talked about him when we were together. She was certain that he loved to hear from us if he ever got our letters, and that he'd write if he ever could, and that he'd send word to us when he could find a way. 'There's no way your dadda would ever give up on us, Siesie,' she said firmly. 'Like there's no way I'll ever give up on him. Samuel loves us as much as we love him. We have to remember that.'

Ten

You Are My Joy

But it was almost a year later that we finally got news about Dad. I was in my last year at school and working hard for my exams – I hoped to get a bursary for my nursing training. One afternoon a friend of Uncle Jimmy's came up to me in the street outside school – I remembered him from the District Six days. He said he'd had a hard job tracking us down.

I explained what had happened to us, and how Mumma had a live-in job. 'So there's only me to talk to today,' I smiled, glad to see someone from the Mbele clan again – we had more or less lost touch with our black family in all the troubles. 'Tell me, Mr Njobe, is there news of Uncle Jimmy? Where is he? Is Mamphela back with him again?'

Mr Njobe took my hand gently in his. 'Be strong, Nomvuyo,' he said. 'I do have news, but it's sad news.

Jimmy is dead. He died last year, in the resettlement camp in the Transkei. And your father, Samuel – he's sick now, too. Very sick. He coughs all the time, and he can't keep food down. It's a bad place where those men were sent.'

At first I couldn't reply, I just stood and stared at this kind, shabbily dressed man, as though I'd lost the power of speech.

'Samuel can't write to you,' he continued, still holding my hand, and patting it gently. 'There's no way he can get paper, and no way to post a letter even if he could. But he got word out to my brother, and my brother told me, and I came to find you.

'Your father sends a message. He says, "you are my joy". He wanted that passed to your mother, and you, and your brothers and sisters.'

I found my voice. 'Is he dying? Is Dad dying?'

Mr Njobe hesitated, but then he patted my hand again and smiled sadly at me. 'I believe he thinks so, Nomvuyo,' he answered gently. 'And from what I hear, it looks like the Lord does, too.'

I went to find Mumma. She was working her shift but I waited for her out the back, and she looked for me in her dinner break. I told her what Mr Njobe had said.

Mumma sat for a long time without speaking, just smoothing her uniform down her knees, over and over, while she stared off into space. Then she squared her shoulders in that old way I remembered – when she'd decided to do something hard and was getting ready to shoulder the burden.

'Siesie, I'm going to do it. I don't care what it takes; I'm going to do it. It's been long enough – too long.'

Suddenly, I knew what she was going to say, and my heart leaped up.

'Mumma, I'm coming with you!'

So we did it.

We went to the Transkei to bring Dad back home.

Eleven

One Trouble At A Time

You'll understand that it wasn't so easy as just say it and do it. It took some working out – just where Dad's camp was and how to get there was only the start of it. But we didn't waste any time, and once we knew where to go we just got on a bus and left. Aunt Lily took care of the little ones for us, and Uncle Yusef guaranteed he'd track Joseph down and get word to him that Dad was coming home. Thinking back now, everyone just assumed we could really do this impossible, unbelievable thing – just like we knew we could.

And the great thing was, it really was *home* that he was coming to! Aunt Lily and Uncle Yusef had told us to bring Dad back to their house in Lavender Street, where they still hung on against the odds, fighting for their rights. They knew he was sick, and they knew it might be something bad like TB, which is highly contagious –

but they still said bring him home. 'We'll deal with it, one trouble at a time,' said Aunt Lily. 'Let's just get Samuel back where he belongs.'

Dad's settlement camp was near a town called Ilinge. We got there late on the third day of travelling – we'd been on buses and two trains and then another bus and we were so tired, with every bone aching. But Mumma wouldn't rest now until we had found Dad, so we just started to walk out along the road from Ilinge, taking turns to carry our suitcase. I remember how I felt that night, how all that walking from Heideveld and back had been nothing; how this walk was the most important one I'd ever done. I was frightened we wouldn't be in time, and worried how we'd get Dad away – but the walking itself kept me going. Step by step: one trouble at a time, like Aunt Lily said.

It was almost dawn by the time we reached the camp, a shabby collection of tin huts in the middle of nothing. It was horrifying. The huts were blazing hot as soon as the sun got up, and there was no shade: no trees, no roads or shops, no electricity, not even any grass. There were whole families living out there sickening and dying on starvation rations, and the land was so arid no one could even grow themselves a few vegetables. The poverty was desperate. It was a desolate, dusty, sandy wasteland.

'These poor men were supposed to farm the land here,' said Mumma, staring around her. 'How could they do that? What could they use? How could they do anything? Oh, my poor Samuel.'

Some children showed us to one of the tin shacks, where we found Dad lying on the ground, wrapped in a dirty old blanket. There was a cup beside him with some water in it. There was nothing else in the hut.

I wouldn't have recognized Dad right away if I hadn't been expecting to see him, he looked so bad. He'd lost so much weight his bones were showing through the skin around his neck and shoulders. His hands were all twisted up – the broken bones had never been tended so they'd set crooked. His face was drawn and grey. And he had a terrible, hacking cough.

But when Mumma knelt down beside him and held the cup to his mouth, and he woke from dozing and opened his eyes and saw her there – well, there aren't words to say how we all felt. Those wasted months fell away, and we were back where we should be: together again.

At first, Dad didn't want to come back with us. He knew he was dying, you see, and he'd fixed in his mind that he didn't want to be a bother. When he'd sent the message that Mr Njobe had given me he'd thought that was it. He'd told us that he loved us one more time, and then he thought he could let go of the world.

But Mumma had other ideas.

Looking back now, I don't know how on earth we got away with it. Dad didn't have a pass to go anywhere at all. He was supposed to stay right where he was; in pain, sick and dying; it didn't matter. And Mumma and I had no right to be there, let alone to take him away. How did we do it?

Well, there was no one in authority around the camp those two days we were there – there was an office but it was closed, and people told us the authorities hadn't been for weeks. So Mumma didn't have to argue with anyone except Dad – and he was too weak to put up much of a fight. Mumma got a taxi to come out from Ilinge, and we all just got into it, and drove to the station. Dad couldn't walk very well, but he could manage slowly if he hung on to my shoulder. So we got him on to the local train, and then a bus, and then the next bus . . . Oh, we had enough sense to go down the coast and then strike inland in short hops, instead of going straight to Cape Town on a long-distance train where we might need to show passes. But even so, we were unbelievably lucky. And no one stopped us. It was like we were invisible.

Dad slept most of the time, which was good because when he was awake he coughed and coughed until he was exhausted, and then he just lay wheezing and gasping for breath. All I could think was that we'd get a doctor when we got back to Lavender Street. And then Dad would get better. One trouble at a time, I said to myself.

The best part was the last part. We made it back to Cape Town, and got off the bus in Sir Lowry Road. Mumma wanted to get a taxi from there, but Dad was feeling so excited to be coming home it gave him a spurt of energy. So we walked, all the way up Tennant Street, and into Hanover Street, and then at last we turned into Lavender Street. Oh, it was sad to pass the gaps where houses had been pulled down, and to see old familiar places boarded up. But it was wonderful just to walk alongside Dad and Mumma, and to turn the corner at the end of Lavender Street and see all the kids sitting waiting on Aunt Lily's *stoep*. Mumma had phoned to say we were almost back, but they were looking for a taxi.

Even Joseph was there and he saw us first. He let out a whoop and then they all came running, Lizzie and Sophie and James. Dad stopped and waited for them with tears pouring down his cheeks. I thought he'd never stop hugging them all, out there in Lavender Street.

We stayed with Dad in Aunt Lily's house until he died, two weeks later. Dad didn't have TB; he'd got a lung infection that had turned to pneumonia because it hadn't been treated, and it was too late for medicine to save him. But he had us all with him for those last weeks, and we had him. He died holding Mumma's hand, and I told myself that had to be enough.

But it was never enough. My family should never have been torn apart. No one's family should be torn apart. My dad should never have been sent away and he should never have died of neglect and in pain. That shouldn't happen to anyone. All this should never have happened. It was wicked, and cruel, and I hated the authorities so much after that, I wanted every one of them to die in pain as well.

No way for a nurse to talk, you might think – and you'd be right. Even Joseph stopped angrily tearing things down in the end, and started building things up instead. And James and Sophie and Lizzie – well they grew up, too, and the new South Africa is an easier place for us all. Not perfect: nothing's perfect. But there is hope for the future now, for people who had no hope.

Nelson Mandela said that no one is born hating another person because of the colour of their skin. He said that people have to learn how to hate, and if they can learn to hate you can teach them how to love – because love comes more naturally to the human heart than hatred does. And if he can believe that, after everything that happened to him, well then, so can I.

I don't hate any more – but I do still ache from carrying all that sadness.

But like I said, we carry *all* our memories in our hearts. So that's where I have District Six and all our happy times there, and my brave father walking back home, down Lavender Street.

Historical Notes

In the years that followed Siesie Ngaba's story there were decades of protest, inside South Africa and around the world, against the apartheid government. In 1990 Nelson Mandela, the leader of the African National Congress and an icon of hope for millions of people, was released from prison after twenty-eight years. Four years later South Africa's first democratic elections were finally held.

The peaceful transition from white rule to a democratic multi-ethnic government in South Africa has been one of the most encouraging events in recent history. In the 'rainbow nation' of the new South Africa, skin colour no longer defines a person or their position in society. The new South African government is trying to transform a country in which millions of its citizens lacked jobs, education, proper housing and civil rights.

The problems are huge, but the spirit of renewal and hope is strong.

In Cape Town, District Six endures in the hearts and memories of those who lived there, and in the District Six museum which is housed in one of the churches. There, a large-scale street map covers the floor, and former residents gather to trace the intricate patterns of their old lives, to archive the rich collection of memorabilia, and to reminisce together.

District Six is also celebrated in a musical, in books and photograph collections, and on film. Pressure continues for the old residents and their descendants to reclaim their heritage. Laws to help house owners reclaim their land have been passed. *District Six Lives!* say the posters. And maybe it will again, one day.

Further Information

If you would like to find out more about South Africa, these books will help:

Fiction:

Beverley Naidoo, *Journey to Jo'burg* (HarperCollins, 1987) This famous book was first published in 1985, but it was banned in South Africa until 1991.

Beverley Naidoo, *Chain of Fire* (HarperCollins, 1989) The sequel to *Journey to Jo'burg* (see above).

Norman Silver, *A Monkey's Wedding* (Faber, 2000) A teenage novel about the new South Africa.

Beverley Naidoo, *No Turning Back* (Puffin, 1996) A novel about street children in the new South Africa.

Non-fiction:

Richard Killeen, *Nelson Mandela* (Hodder Wayland, 1998)

Nelson Mandela, *Long Walk to Freedom* – Children's version (Little, Brown, 2001)

Glossary

Afrikaans A language spoken by many South Africans, developed from the Dutch that the Boer settlers spoke.

Apartheid The Afrikaans word for 'separateness'. It was the system of controlling different ethnic groups that secured and maintained white domination in South Africa.

Boere The plural of *Boer*, the Afrikaans word for white South Africans descended from the Dutch settlers.

Democratic A system of government in which free elections are held, and all adults can vote.

Deported Sent away against your will, for political reasons.

Koe'susters A shortened form of '*koeksusters*', an Afrikaans word for a traditional kind of doughnut developed in Cape Town.

Mealies Maize (sweet corn). From the Afrikaans word *mielie*. The ground meal is made into porridge.

Sjambok A flexible cane, used by the South African police in apartheid times.

Skollie An Afrikaans slang word for a hooligan or a gangster.

Stoep An Afrikaans word for the broad platform step in front of a house. The plural of *Stoep* is *Stoepe*.

Township The separate areas outside main South African towns for different ethnic groups. Almost all non-white people in cities were forcibly removed to townships, during the apartheid years.

Umvubo An African dish made from mealies and sour milk.

Xhosa The language of the Xhosa peoples, who lived in South Africa many years before the white settlers arrived.

THE STAR HOUSES

Stewart Ross

Snipping away the stitching that held on my yellow star, my mother said defiantly, 'Right! That's simple. From now on we won't wear these silly badges. None of us!' When she had finished, she exclaimed, 'There! Now you're just an ordinary Hungarian like everyone else.' If only it had been that simple.

Bandi Guttmann is a fourteen-year-old Hungarian Jew, living in Budapest in 1944. German forces have occupied the city and life for Bandi and his family is about to become unbearable. Set apart from the rest of the Hungarian community, and denied basic human rights, the family's only weapon is their determination to survive. But in the face of mindless hatred, will the Guttmanns' strength, love and courage be enough to hold them together?

The Star Houses is based on the memoirs of Andor Guttmann.

THE WATER PUPPETS

Clive Gifford

Seven white crosses . . . Seven men dead. Xuan shuddered at the thought. What was the point of such death? Seven soldiers must have died right here on this deserted, lonely road. 'Why?' Xuan wondered to himself.

The farmers of Noy Thien village have enough of a war on their hands with the seasons, the monsoon and the soil – they have no reason to fight anything else. But this is Vietnam and it's 1967. The country is divided and American troops have moved in. For thirteen-year-old Xuan and his family, their world is about to be turned upside down. Neighbours are fighting each other and no one is certain who the real enemy is. Can life for Xuan's family ever be the same again?

Another Survivors title from Hodder Wayland

THE ENEMY

James Riordan

It was so pitiful to see. Now and then we'd hear the screaming Stukas diving on these poor, defenceless souls, like eagles on their prey. The sky would be black with them. And they'd send the refugees diving into ditches or under wagons. Why, oh, why did they have to gun down old men, women and children?

War brings out the worst in some people, and the best in others. It's spring 1940 in occupied France when Marie and her mother find themselves looking after two injured soldiers. But one is English and the other is German, and they are sworn enemies. The two patients must not find out about each other. Will the compassion and understanding of one girl and her mother be enough to keep the peace?

ORDER FORM

Other titles in the SURVIVORS series:

0 7502 3311 7 THE STAR HOUSES: A Story from the Holocaust   £9.99 ❑
       Stewart Ross
0 7502 3528 4 THE WATER PUPPETS: A Story from Vietnam   £9.99 ❑
       Clive Gifford
0 7502 3442 3 THE ENEMY: A Story from World War II   £9.99 ❑
       James Riordan
0 7502 3630 2 BROKEN LIVES: A Victorian Mine Disaster   £9.99 ❑
       Neil Tonge

All Hodder Children's books are available at your local bookshop or newsagent, or can be ordered direct from the publisher. Just tick the titles you want and fill in the form below. Prices and availability subject to change without notice.

Hodder Wayland, Cash Sales Department, Bookpoint, 130 Milton Park, Abingdon, OXON, OX14 4TD, UK. If you have a credit card, our call team would be delighted to take your order by telephone. Our direct line is *01235 400414* (lines open 9.00 am–6.00 pm Monday to Saturday, 24 hour message answering service). Alternatively you can send a fax on *01235 400454*.

Or please enclose a cheque or postal order made payable to Bookpoint Ltd to the value of the cover price and allow the following for postage and packing:
UK & BFPO – £1.00 for the first book, 50p for the second book, and 30p for each additional book ordered up to a maximum charge of £3.00.
OVERSEAS & EIRE – £2.00 for the first book, £1.00 for the second book, and 50p for each additional book.

Name ....

Address ....

....

....

If you would prefer to pay by credit card, please complete:
Please debit my Visa/Access/Diner's Card/American Express (delete as applicable) card no:

Signature ....

Expiry Date ....